Rise Up

A Stilter's Adventures in Higher Consciousness

Published by Mercury Press International
405 Santa Anita Rd.
Santa Barbara, CA 93105
www.MercuryPress.com

Library of Congress Cataloging-in-Publication Data

McGinnes, Marc, 1941- author.
Rise Up: A Stilter's Adventures in Higher Consciousness/Marc McGinnes
ISBN-13: 978-0-9990342-0-0
BISAC: Body and Mind - Inspiration and Personal Growth

First Printing: June 2017

Marc McGinnes

Rise Up
A Stilter's Adventures in Higher Consciousness

Mercury Press International

Santa Barbara - California

to our higher selves

Marc at 2016 Santa Barbara Solstice Parade. Photo: Ronald L. Williams

FOREWORD

"Go High" is not just a great political slogan, it's the way my friend Marc McGinnes lives life.

Over the years, I've had the great privilege to work as a theatre director. Many extraordinary plays begin with a prologue. This sharpens the audience's senses and informs them how to look and listen to the upcoming play. This is what Marc has been doing for Santa Barbara every June for as long as I can remember.

When I hear the rumble of Solstice drums and wend my way through the gathering crowds I know the first thing I want to do is find Marc standing oh so tall near the beginning of the Summer Solstice Parade. He is the prologue! Marc's always smiling and always joyfully sharing his unique perspective on what's ahead and what's coming up behind him. When I yell out and catch his attention, he puts his hand to his heart and smiles back with our shared history. I hope this book inspires some to join him and breathe in the rarified air up there.

Peace and love,

Jenny Sullivan
Board Member of The Mime Caravan, creator of
The Summer Solstice Celebration of Santa Barbara

Photo: John Barron

LOVE AT FIRST SIGHT

When I first saw stilts in 1975, it was love at first sight. I saw a man who worked on stilts, painting the ceiling in a building being remodeled in my downtown Santa Barbara neighborhood. He told me they saved him from having to climb up and down ladders all the time. He seemed so relaxed, totally at ease as he laughed, talked, and worked on stilts. I immediately saw the celebratory potential in these babies, and I asked him if I could put them on.

From the moment I stood up with the stilts strapped to my legs, I was hooked. I was 33 years old, trim, fit, strong, and possessed of all the athletic abilities that had enabled me to be an outstanding player in several sports during my years at Stanford and Berkeley. I realized that stilts offered a wide-open opportunity to blaze new trails in a whole new sport. I took my first few steps on those borrowed stilts, and saw how easy it would be for me to master the use of these devices. I knew at once that stilts would become an important part of my life. I found out where to get them, and immediately sent away for my own pair.

Sure enough, I quickly learned to walk and even boogie around on my stilts. I strolled around at increasing distances on the sidewalks around the neighborhood, becoming more and more confident in my movements. What fun it was! People were amazed to see such a sight, and I had wonderful conversations and contacts with them. Our joy was contagious and uplifting.

Made of aluminum, this first pair of stilts strapped onto the leg at the calf, and the height of the footplate was adjustable between one and three feet. I paid 99 dollars and 99 cents for them. In those days, that was a substantial sum, but I still consider it to be the best investment I ever made in terms of joy to the dollar. My value, the value of me to myself, increased substantially when I first rose up. It will not diminish when I set my stilts aside, for I have learned that we can be on stilts in our bare feet. It's my fervent hope that you, dear reader, will be moved by this book to make a similar investment in joy, and make strides into your own higher consciousness on stilts.

1. GETTING HIGH

Although there are certain risks involved, stilting itself is easy. I love being able to put that ease on display. Stilting is simple because a stilt is simply a riser, a device upon which the stilter stands. Because the technology is so basic, stilts go back thousands, perhaps millions of years. The story of our presence on the planet is far longer than the short version that written history provides. Our ancestors in the early Stone Age were making stone tools a couple of million years before our Bronze Age ancestors learned to devise systems of writing to record the events and stories of their lives and times.

In these prehistoric (literally "before history") times, our ancestors were doing their best to hunt and gather sufficient food, and to secure adequate shelter to keep themselves alive. We know that they made tools for various purposes, and I think we can logically suppose that the elementary notion of stilting was invented around this time. Using materials from trees, bamboo, bone and hide, they could have made stilts as tools in order to rise up and reach higher resources, pass over obstacles, see farther, and generally do the work necessary to

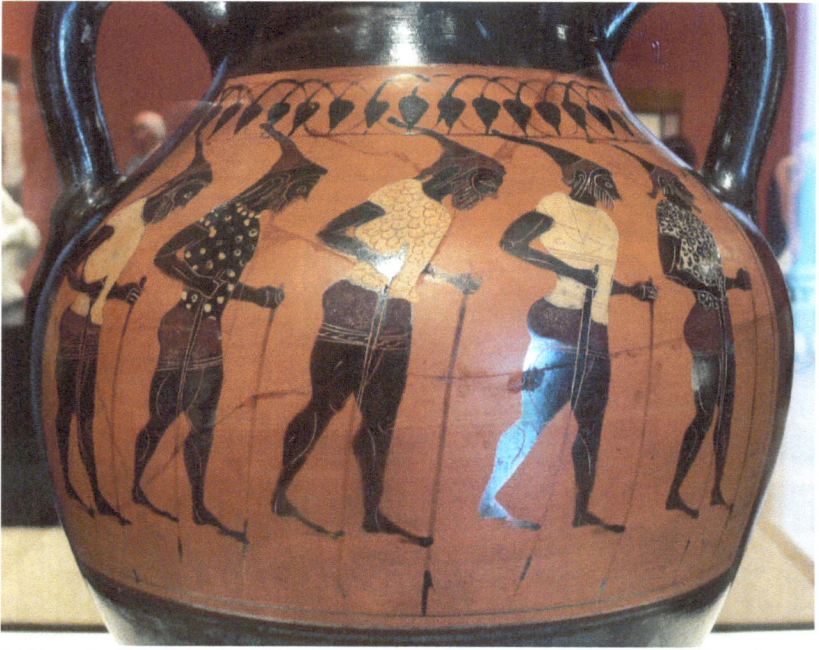

Stilters depicted on Greek storage jar (550-525 BCE). Photo: Remi Matthis, James Logie Memorial Collection, University of Canterbury, New Zealand

their survival. When our stilting ancestors developed agriculture and domesticated livestock in the late Stone Age (around 10,000 BCE), they rose up on stilts as useful tools for working in orchards, fields, and grazing terrain.

By the time our human family passed from the prehistoric era to the time of recorded history, stilts and stilting were known to people living in places all over the world. Some of them began to use stilts for ceremonial purposes and joyful play, and not only as tools with which to perform work. Evidence of this can be seen today in artifacts such as the ancient Greek storage jar from the sixth century BCE (pictured above), depicting a group of stilting figures engaged in some kind of ceremony or celebration.

If you want to learn more about traditions of stilting around the world, I heartily recommend S. Carl Hirsch's book *Stilts* (Viking Press, 1972). It's a gem for young people that tells stories and "tall tales" about how stilts have been used for work and play throughout history, right up to today, by people living in Asia, Africa, Europe, the South Seas, and the Americas. It's out of print, but is worth seeking

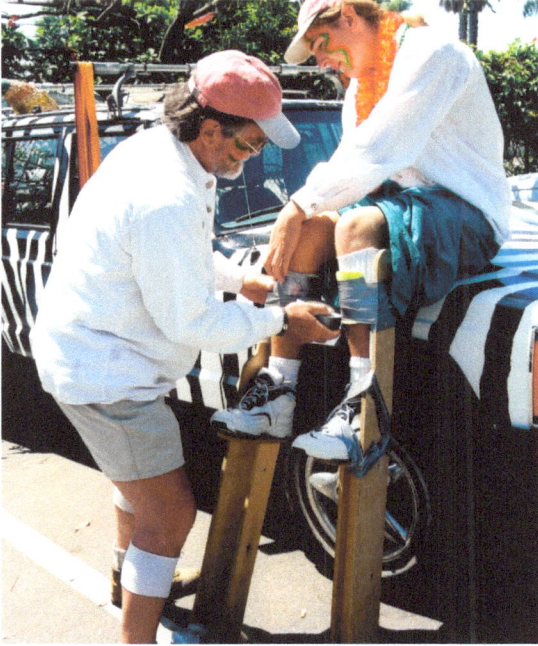

Strapping Zach into his stilts. Photo: Kathy Snow

out. Until a new edition is published, it will take some determined and fortunate rising up to acquire.

I also happily recommend that you do an online search for "stilts and stilting." I think you'll be amazed by the number of fascinating hits that show the extent to which people living in places all over the world have risen up on stilts from prehistoric times to the present. The internet is also a great place to find your own pair of stilts, and join the stilting tradition yourself.

Today, you can find quite a range of sizes and weights of stilts out there. Personally, I have really taken advantage of this abundance. I am the Imelda Marcos of stilts. Over the years, I have purchased and commissioned the fabrication of numerous pairs of stilts. At present, I have six pairs of metal stilts, and a dozen pairs of wooden stilts, some of which I've made myself. Over the course of my stilting career, the height of my stilts has ranged from 36 inches to the current 24 inches. Whenever I get a new pair, I have to take the time to experiment a bit and get used to securing myself into them.

I've taught hundreds of people to walk on stilts, and the first order of business is just overcoming a natural fear of falling. However, there's no real reason to fall, as long as you're secure upon the stilt. If they're worn properly, you will be secure. The kind of stilts I have fasten to my calf. You may use a strap, Velcro, or even duct tape to fasten yourself into your stilts. For many years, stilters in my family used duct tape, but I've recently developed a preference for Velcro straps, which provide a firm, lightweight fix and a speedy way of getting on and off the stilts. When I teach people how to walk on stilts, I do the strapping in myself, and I emphasize the importance of being securely strapped. You can't have any wobbliness between your leg and the piece of the stilt running up along the outside of your calf, or any wobbliness where your shoe sits on top of the standing platform.

As simple as stilts are, they still require some maintenance, and it's of great importance to maintain your stilts in good working order. It's disastrous to suffer a breakdown. Once I had a breakdown during the Santa Barbara Solstice parade. One of my stilts completely broke when a bolt sheared off inside it. When I felt it, I stopped immediately. Fortunately I didn't collapse on the leg with the broken stilt. If my weight had shifted at that moment, off I would have gone, unprepared for a terrible fall. It would have been a catastrophe, but for my great good fortune. So I always check very carefully to make sure my stilts are in good shape. Perfection in all things cannot be guaranteed, so there is always a certain amount of risk of mechanical breakdown. The idea is to minimize that risk whenever possible. I suppose it's like flying an airplane: if you're gonna fly, you'd better do everything in your power to ensure that your plane works as intended. I enjoy taking risks to perform at my highest level, but I take care to respect the dangers, and to anticipate and avoid them to the best of my ability.

I always recognize the possibility that I could fall, but I'm not afraid of it, though perhaps I ought to be. Indeed, I have fallen a few times. One year in the parade, I fell on the pavement, breaking a finger and injuring my wrist. The worst part of it was that I frightened my granddaughter Helena, who was on her stilts in the parade for the first time.

I tripped and fell down right in front of her. I got up, with the help of my son Skye, and I went on and finished. I'm so grateful that I was fortunate enough to be able to finish. Sadly, Helena

Stilting debut of Helena McGinnes. Photo: Eric Isaacs/EMI Photography

hasn't been on stilts since then, and I regret that my carelessness may have caused that. Yet in general, avoiding a fall on stilts is much easier than avoiding one elsewhere in life. And if—despite your best efforts—you do fall, there's a way of falling that optimizes your chances of avoiding injury to yourself and others. Wouldn't it be wonderful if such a technique existed in the fields of work or romance?

Once I fell after the parade, when the after-parade ceremonies were held in the grassy area in the courtyard of the Santa Barbara County Courthouse. The celebrants were dancing around in there, and I put my foot into a hole around a sprinkler head. Usually I'm very careful when I'm up on stilts, careful not to fall, and therefore careful not to trip or to allow others to become hazards by running into me. But I didn't see this sprinkler hole because I was looking down at the view of all the beautiful young women dancing in halter tops... I was distracted, to say the least.

Another time, I actually performed a superhuman feat. Rather than falling, I flew! I was in Alameda Park, and the parade was over. I was exhausted, and I came to join my family on a blanket on the grass. As I was getting ready to descend, I stumbled, nearly falling on all of them. In the instant of my recognition that this was about to happen, I flexed my legs and kicked myself forward, as if diving from a dock into a body of water. My weight and the metal part of the stilts cleared my family, and at the last instant I squeezed my legs together, bent my knees, and brought the bottoms of the stilts together and skyward, so as to avoid hitting anyone. It was a miracle. I wish someone had it on tape. A man flying on stilts!

I'm grateful that this brief flight—and unexpected landing—took place on grass, because grass is a much more forgiving surface than asphalt or concrete. You should definitely learn to stilt on grass, not on a hard surface. Before you get up on stilts, stand comfortably and practice falling forward. As your body comes forward, assume a crouching position, and get ready to use your arms as shock absorbers. Keep your elbows bent and your wrists loose, so your face, torso, and knees won't slam into the ground. Refer to the illustration below to see how this translates into a controlled fall on stilts. Just practice falling like that, because if you must fall, that's the direction you want to go: always fall forward. If you begin to fall back, twist yourself so you can fall forward. Again, practice that before you're on stilts. Begin falling as if you're going to fall back, but twist your body around so that you fall face down instead. It's counter-intuitive, but it's really important, because the risk of injury is much more serious if you fall on your back.

That's the worst case scenario: falling is the worst thing that could happen. What you generally find is that you're not going to fall, because stilting is easy. Of course, you do need to be careful. You need to watch out for things you might trip on as you step over them, and you need to make sure you lift your feet up sufficiently to clear any obstacles. You also need to watch out for people, animals, bicycles and other things moving around you, depending on where you are.

When I'm teaching someone to use stilts for the first time, we'll stand up together on the grass. At first, I hold their hand, and I'll assure them that we're not in a hurry. They get to decide when they're ready to take the first step. So we wait, and within a very short time, the new stilter takes a first step, a second step, a third step, and very soon—almost every time—I hear some version of "Hey, this is easy!" as if they didn't believe me when I told them how easy it would be. In the case of my ten-year-old grandson and friends, it was literally off to the races. They immediately began to run on the stilts. If you're going to run on stilts—particularly if you're an adult, as only small, light folks can get away with running on ordinary stilts—get some kangaroo stilts. They have springs and are designed for loping along like a gazelle.

Whether you're a beginner or an accomplished stilter, it's always a good idea to have a spotter. Your spotter should be a stilter, because they'll better understand what's involved in the process for you and for them. A spotter should be somebody of an appropriate size who has the ability and good judgment to help keep you upright if you're about to fall. They should also have the judgment to know not to get in your way when you're unavoidably falling, so that you're able to fall properly.

You may wish to carry a staff until you are ready to fly free. It can be helpful for maintaining balance, and you can lean on it from time to time if you get tired and want to take a quick break. In a celebratory or ceremonial context, a staff can be decorative. Sometimes in the Solstice Parade I have a staff with ribbons on it, but sometimes I go without a staff so I can have my hands free to spin poi. In Santa

The right way to fall on stilts.

Barbara, bamboo is plentiful, and because it's strong but lightweight it makes an ideal stilting staff. When I'm up there, I like to make big gestures with my arms and hands, and using a staff can be part of that fun. The gestures convey my gratitude for being alive and in joy in the presence of the wonderful people who are in the parade and who are watching the parade, beaming appreciation and support.

I also used to put silver in my dark beard and streak silver in my dark hair. Now my beard is white, as is my hair, so I have no need to do any streaking of that kind anymore. Getting old on stilts is pretty much like getting old on your feet. It's really not all that much fun, but it's the way it is, and it gives us an opportunity to keep moving along in as much grace and beauty as we can muster.

I'm now clearly past my prime, but even when I was in the bloom of youthful fitness there were times when I had to play as an athlete while I was hurt. I learned how to compensate for injuries in one way or another, and in most cases I was able to play through temporary afflictions. Yet old age is something more than a temporary affliction, isn't it?

So I ask myself, "How I can compensate for the condition of my body as it is today?" I wonder how to play through the pain in the generally weaker muscles and ligaments of my legs, my balky and arthritic left knee, and my feet damaged by peripheral neuropathy. The saving grace is that I still have the essential sense of balance. For this gift, I am grateful.

I can compensate in three ways. First, I train for stilting, as if it were an athletic event. I'm not a fitness fanatic, but I do consider myself a lifelong athlete. I do daily walking and conditioning exercises, sometimes together with other stilters, but mostly on my own. I regularly swim and kayak in the ocean. I shed extra weight, and keep myself as strong and limber as possible. Second, I make sure my stilts are suitable to my circumstances. Today they're shorter and lighter than other stilts I've worn. Third, I have to pace myself to make sure that I have enough energy to make it all the way from the beginning of the parade to the end.

Growing old on stilts requires taking things slower and easier than before. In doing so, I must be mindful, concerning how my spirit moves my body to express its joy. Forty, thirty, twenty, even fifteen years ago, I never had to be concerned about my ability to be in full dancing mode up the ten blocks of the parade route and on into the park for a few more hours of dancing and cavorting. I used to dance the whole way, spinning around, making all the movements to the beat of the dance. Those days are gone. Now I move at a slower pace, dancing to a longer beat, pausing to rest from time to time. I drink plenty of water. I walk with a spotter nearby, who can provide drinking water, emergency assistance, and steadying encouragement and support.

I turned 75 years old last year, and I still walked and danced on stilts in the Santa Barbara Summer Solstice Parade. I've done it nearly every year for the past four decades, missing it only for reasons of medical necessity. I don't consider my advancing years to be such a reason, even though my doctor thinks me foolish to want to prolong my life on stilts. My diagnosis of his condition is that he doesn't understand what it's like to be hooked on higher consciousness.

Photo: Bob Evans 2017

2. HIGHER CONSCIOUSNESS

Stilts provide an incomparable high. I don't just mean a physical high, but a mental, emotional, and spiritual high. For about the first 20 years of my stilting adventures in the Summer Solstice Parade, I would be up on this high for as long as six or seven hours. It was an unsurpassed mechanical high, and it was hard for me to come down. Despite the exhaustion I'd feel when it was over, being high was a magnificent experience. It isn't an artificial high. I'm in love up there, and it's not artificial to want to love everyone. It's a blessed state of bliss and mindful awareness. You could also call it "being in the zone," because of that greater awareness of the present moment. It's as if there really is a zone of joy just above our heads, a place we're able to enter when we rise up on stilts.

Accessing that zone or state is a spiritual practice. Well, all life is spiritual practice, and some practices are—to a given individual— more interesting than others. For me, stiltwalking is one of my favorite spiritual practices, a means of rising up into higher consciousness. When I'm on stilts, I become my higher self, a being who breathes in and beams out light and love, and who can unselfconsciously perform awe-inspiring expressions of joy. It's me at my best, as loving and generous as I can be. I know that I am my most unselfish when I am up there on my stilts, giving it everything that I can to bring good tidings, joy, encouragement and inspiration. I mean it when I say I feel like I'm in heaven up there, and that I'm intimately connected with everyone and everything I see. It's an opportunity to let spirit be the guide, the voice, and the expression of what one is. When I am up on stilts I find that I'm able to express wondrously well the love of life that I feel welling up and overflowing. I'm gushing, I'm breathing in the attention directed at me, and I'm giving back, breathing out my attention and my regard, and it's nourishing. It's my spirit's essence

Zach uplifted in the Solstice Parade. Photo: Pete Evans

that I'm giving forth, breathing out, extending. I experience a transcendent connection with others all along the parade route.

This state is accessible to anyone. I've observed the same phenomenon in my sons and in other people on stilts who are really into it, really giving, really celebrating. When people see that, something of the same quality opens up in them, and they start beaming out this joy. So my experience in all these years has been that of being carried along up the parade route, carried along by joy. If you're gonna be in higher consciousness, spread joy. Sing joy to the world with your body, mind, and spirit. Sing joy to the world with all your might, for all you're worth.

My performances on stilts express that experience of being alight with joy, gratitude, and radiant reverence. I dress in a way that seems appropriate to this expression of ecstasy, and sometimes people watching the parade interpret this in an interesting way. One year a man in the crowd along the parade route called out, "Are you auditioning for the role of God?" He was grinning broadly—obviously enjoying himself—and his tone was not at all challenging. "You look just like I imagine him to be." We both laughed. I could see why

Church on time. Photo: Kathy Snow

he asked the question, since I was dressed in white, with a wreath that might have seemed to be either a halo or, I suppose, a crown of thorns. I didn't intend blaspheme, to portray God or a god-like figure, but I know that some people saw me in that light, and I was happy that what people saw in me gave them joy.

We'd all like to be perceived as our higher selves. Stilting allows me to stand out as I wish to be seen and remembered. Yet I didn't fall in love with stilting because I merely wanted to stand out. Stilting is fun, it's something that you can enjoy by yourself, without any observer. It's really fun to be physically that high, and to move along and see the world from that height. Of course it takes some ego to get up there, but it takes some ego to do anything.

Stilts aren't tools of egotism. They change your relationship to others in a way that's completely different from being off on an ego trip. When I'm up there above everyone, I'm also seeing them (for the most part) at their best. The experience of seeing people at their best is wonderfully uplifting in itself. When people look up at me, what they see is a person beaming appreciation and encouragement, expressing neighborly affection in every gesture. There isn't a single bone of judgment in my whole, super-tall body, and that's one of the reasons I so love being on stilts: to completely get free from the judgmental inclinations of my mind, to rise above them. I'm impersonating a human being standing taller than others, and yet not standing "over" them in any sense that diminishes them or elevates me at their expense. When I rise up on stilts I can see most clearly that we are all uplifted when we take joy in being with each other.

So what I do when I'm on stilts in this state of joy is to lift, but it's a mutual lifting that comes from the exchange or multiplication of joy. Being on stilts is uplifting for me, and in that state, I wish to uplift others and I have the capability to do so. In turn they uplift me, and the cycle of joy continues. As I am lifted, I lift! And my intention to lift enables me to be lifted. That's why I feel as if I've been carried up the parade route, because I've been lifted by the people who take joy in my joy, in seeing me. Together we're all getting higher, rising higher and higher into joy as I'm breezing along on stilts, riding the undulations of spiritual energies, the earth's uprising.

You should see the looks you get when you're on stilts. Eyes brimming with wonder, the child's eyes in the faces of people, regardless of their ages. When you're on stilts, you see the beautiful child in adults, and that's a wonderful thing. My favorite incident of this phenomenon occurred in 1979, at the famous "No Nukes" rally in San Luis Obispo at which 30,000 people protested against the proposed Diablo Canyon nuclear plant. The event had been organized by the Abalone Alliance, one of the Environmental Defense Center's first clients, and I and other EDC attorneys and staff members were there in support. Governor Jerry Brown helicoptered in with his

"No Nukes" rally near Diablo Canyon, 1979.
Photo: Grace Moceri

then-girlfriend Linda Ronstadt, who performed in the rock concert from a hastily-constructed bandstand in a large field on which thousands of people were milling around.

I was on my stilts, walking along on this beautiful day, and though the ground was a bit uneven—pocked with ground squirrel holes here and there—I was relaxed and in a place of joy. In front of me were five Hell's Angels, five tough guys in all the regalia, "Hell's Angels" emblazoned on the backs of their jackets, the whole nine yards. Facing me were their five girlfriends. At first they were at some distance, but as I got close to them the women looked up, one by one, to the point where the men noticed that their women were taking their eyes off of them and looking over their heads. So they turned around, maybe a little surprised, a little angry, but as soon as they saw me, they were utterly transfigured. They became five little angels with faces of rapt wonderment, five little boys, saying "Oh, wow!" because I was beaming at them, and I had my hands outstretched, ribbons coming off of me in all directions, all dressed in white and eight feet tall. They might have thought they'd gone to heaven. The little boy in each one of them just shone out. And the women saw their men's response, and they all laughed, and we shared a great moment of fellowship and closeness. It nearly knocked me back off my stilts, I nearly fell down, it was so beautiful and powerful.

That was the first big blast I received to tell me that this was a great way to give something, and a reward for sharing that higher consciousness. On stilts, you can be this incredibly powerful being. If your intention is to be in joy and be loving, you can shine your love on people and receive a tremendous response. You can receive the gift of their amazement, wonder, and childish delight. I've never had a person look at me that way when I'm just wearing my shoes.

3. HIGH TIMES

Once you've experienced higher consciousness on stilts, you'll always be looking for opportunities to share it. I've had the great good fortune to be part of the Santa Barbara Summer Solstice Parade almost from its inception, and I couldn't ask for a better opportunity to share the joy of stilting. The parade is a stilter's paradise. Talk about fun! Can you picture yourself dancing along fearlessly, comfortably, and joyfully, in the midst of throngs of smiling uplifted faces, in the joyous din of the celebration? Others dreamed it, and rose up to make it a reality.

The event was started in 1974 by Michael Gonzales, a painter and mime who lived in Santa Barbara. On the occasion of his birthday, Michael and a group of his friends from the Mime Caravan walked up State Street, dancing up the sidewalks with banners and colorful ribbons. It was so much fun that those of us who weren't there heard about it, and it was decided that it would become a larger event the following year. They decided to march up the street, and acquired a permit from the city to do so. That launched these wonderful annual events, in which the whole community is welcome to participate. I've been in all of them since 1975, except 2015, when I was unable even to attend the parade because I was laid up in bed with hurt legs.

I took part in the first Summer Solstice Parade to which the general public was invited. At that time I was living at 1005 Santa Barbara Street, above my law office, with a yard next door and our organic garden on the side. My son Skye was living there part-time with me. In those early years of the parade, we would simply walk the short distance to the start of the parade at Cota and State, and take off from there. There were no badges, there was no real organization, we just went up the street, and figured it out on the spot. I loved that spontaneity, and I loved the excitement of walking down to the start of the parade, getting people involved. We only had six short blocks to go, but we set out plenty early because we knew we'd be stopping and talking to everyone along the way.

On my stilts, I walked and danced up the parade route, carrying a long bamboo pole festooned with ribbons in the colors of the rainbow. I dressed in flowing white, wearing a loosely-fitting white cotton top. There were wings sewn under the arms, so when I spread my arms it looked like I had wings, and a rainbow of ribbons sewn around my neck. A garland of interwoven flowers atop my head of long hair, my face and hands painted

Marc in the 1975 Summer Solstice Parade. Photo: John Barron

with golden glitter, I moved among the parade participants and paused frequently to dip my rainbow ribbons into the midst of the spectators.

At that time the route headed up State Street to Anapamu Street, passing under the courthouse archway on Anacapa Street, and ending in the sunken garden for hours of dancing and cavorting on the lawn. When participants and spectators joined together in the garden, I remained on my stilts, dancing to the music of the bands and the drum circle that were a part of the ongoing festivities. I was a magnet for smiling faces and joyful people expressing good wishes, asking about how it was to be up and playing around on stilts. Our family and friends had a place staked out with blankets and an ice chest or two, and we'd hang out there for several hours, enjoying and participating in the scene. Several times parents presented their small children for me to hold and speak with as we looked out across the sea of joyful people. I had conversations with children who wanted to know if I was a real giant, and how I grew to be so tall. "By eating lots of vegetables and fruits and other healthy foods... And by wearing these stilts," I said, while lifting my pant leg to reveal the metal contraptions underneath.

Extra-long pants are a key part of my stilting getup. I used those original canvas drawstring pants for many years. I still have 'em.

They're antique stilt pants now, or at least vintage stilt pants. I had them made by the seamstress at Santa Barbara City College in the costume department of the theatre program. I asked her for something like a 36-inch waist and 56-inch inseam. We had a good laugh over those measurements. She saw me in the parade that year and called out to me, and we had a nice exchange.

I always did my utmost to respond personally to the great many people along the parade route who called out to me. I strode or danced over to the side of the street where they were sitting or standing, gesturing respectfully and joyfully to them, sometimes sharing a few words. At some times there have been lots of people calling out, because I've often been visible in the community for my work as an environmental leader and activist. I also taught popular courses at UCSB, attended by many students who then took pleasure in seeing their teacher in this context, which was, to say the least, unusual.

After being in the parade so many years, I'm often approached by people about it when I'm just doing my everyday business in public. Standing in the express line at Trader Joe's, a woman recognized me, and what came out of her mouth was "Weren't you the famous Marc McGinnes who was on stilts in the Summer Solstice Parade?" I replied, "I am the famous Marc McGinnes who was on stilts in the Summer Solstice Parade!"

Yet she was more correct, for I am no longer famous. I may think of myself in the same way, but I am no longer famous in the way that she described, and that's a plain fact. I *was* famous! I was the attorney who had so much fun being in the parade and including people who were watching, inviting and appreciating their participation, their enthusiasm and receptivity. I gave myself to joy publicly, and in so doing enabled others to find their spot in joy. Hundreds of times, people have said to me, "Don't I know you? You seem awfully familiar... Oh, you're the man on stilts!"

In a sense, my stilting has taken over the rest of my public identity. At one point in my legal career I was in the newspaper all the time. I pioneered the field of environmental law, and my colleagues and I turned back a lot of development. It was newsworthy. I took pleasure in the fact that I was doing work that was worthy of note, and I considered it a part of my good citizenship to do these things. I sacrificed income for the satisfaction of doing this kind of work in the public interest. It feels good to see your name in the paper in association with something you believe in. Even when I was a kid, I loved getting my name in the paper as a little baseball player, because I wanted to be the next Mickey Mantle. My ego was more attached to my work as an environmental lawyer, but I learned that people recognized me as the man on stilts instead.

Early on in my career, I asked myself if I wanted to be known more for being the man on stilts than for my environmental work. My first response when I began to be recognized as the man on stilts was to say, "No, I'm the guy in the paper who just successfully stopped that development down on Hammonds Meadow... Are you thinking of that?" Heck no, they weren't thinking of that, they were interested in the man on stilts! "God, I love that!" they would gush. "Is it easy? Are you afraid you're gonna fall?"

Recently, a man who's watched every parade since the very beginning said to me, "Oh, you're the man on stilts?" His wife, by the way, works at the Environmental Studies program at UCSB, which I helped to develop, but he couldn't quite place me as being from that part of his life.

I came to realize that it really doesn't matter, because it's part and parcel of the same thing, which is serving the community. Being this man on stilts was an important part of the performance that we—the solstice celebrants—were doing as members of the artistic community in Santa Barbara. I consider that I actually have a responsibility to be the man on stilts, because people let me know when I don't fulfill it. When I wasn't there in 2015, I heard about it. "Hey, we didn't see you on stilts, what's happening?" people asked. "Everything alright, is everything OK?"

"The man on stilts" appears in the mural of the Summer Solstice Celebration now on the parking garage in the rear of the Granada Theatre. There are three pieces to the mural, painted by Ben Bottoms and Richard McLaughlin. There I am, the stilt man, and I have an old picture of myself in front of that mural in its original location on the side of the Earthling Bookstore. I'm happy to be identified with this role, which has its origin in the creative spirit of the community.

Last summer at a party for the Solstice Workshop, there was a show of hands to see how many people had been doing the parade for different lengths of time. We saw a show of hands for all the people

"The man on stilts" in front of his depiction in Summer Solstice Celebration mural. Photo: Kathy Snow

doing the parade for 20 years, and many hands went up. 30 years? A few hands went up. 40 years? Joan Melendez and I raised our hands. We were the only two. That was a meaningful moment, being invited to raise my hand as an elder, as a person who had done this for so many years. That night, over the course of a couple of hours, I was able to share in simple interactions, dancing, talking, listening, feeling a kinship and a bond for which I am grateful.

So it's with great reluctance that I consider the prospect of having to curtail my stilting in the face of advancing age. I dread the thought of putting the stilts aside forever, but I'll need to know when to stop. I've seen a white-haired woman in the Fiesta Parade who appeared to be strapped onto her saddle atop her large and beautiful horse. She didn't look particularly at ease or happy with this arrangement, and I'm not surprised, because I've heard the legend of this woman. In her prime, she was a bold, flame-haired beauty, a masterful horsewoman and a highlight of the parade. She had a wild streak, and they say that more than once she rode her horse right into the old Joe's Cafe. The horse reared up over the bar, scattering the crowd, and she rode back out of the place with a whoop and a cry of "Viva la Fiesta!"

They say that in past parades she was dynamite, beautiful, sparky, zesty, calling out to the crowd, sitting high in the saddle, wearing a beautiful dress, in exaltation of her joy. I imagine that's how she wants to be remembered. I want to be remembered for the years I danced the whole route—and partied for hours afterwards—in my highest stilts.

I'm afraid of getting to the point where I'm just going through the motions. I don't want people to say, "Look at this old fart struggling up the street on stilts! How embarrassing, I hope he doesn't fall over and kill himself." Then my stilting days will be done, and I will bring my joy to ground level, and spread it there. I'll be part of the stilts group, but I'll do my lifting from the pavement, because the important thing is to continue to participate lovingly in my community.

I know I'm getting close to making this change, because last year, though I made it through the whole parade route, I pretty much staggered across the finish line. I gave all I had along the way. My wreath was crooked, and I nearly fell more than once, but I loved being there. I challenged myself to do what I loved, and I did it in a way that was loving to all concerned. At the end, my sons Skye and Zach were both there, and they both took me in their loving care, helping me come to the end, to sit down and take off the stilts.

Stilts have been such an enjoyable part of my life in Santa Barbara. Stilting is a wonderful way of being in joy and spreading the joy that I feel. I wish to carry on in the joyful spirit of Michael Gonzales, whose birthday celebration was the event that started the parade. I think it's time to dance on stilts at the beginning and at the end, but in the middle, I'll leave the stilting to others. After all, I'm only one part of a big parade.

Being with other stiltwalkers has been interesting. I've seen some really fine stiltwalkers. One fellow, I think he was from Australia, a young, lithe man, could actually somersault—can you believe it?—on stilts. In a group of stilters from San Luis Obispo, I saw a fellow riding the kind of stilts on which the feet are just the poles, circular poles probably three or four inches in diameter. They require you to constantly shift your weight, even while standing more or less in place. He was a young dancer, Latino, I think, and he would come parading in an Aztec kind of costume. Garbed in gold and red, he was a skilled stiltwalker and a beautiful sight to behold.

I have coached others who will take my place. I've done stilts workshops for children, and at the age of 74, I coached Ralph Luikart, who is 71! Ralph is a rookie stilter and a new friend, who told me he dreamed of being with me on stilts in the Summer Solstice Parade. In training, we met at La Playa Stadium and walked the steps. 72 rows of seats from top to bottom, bottom to top, up and down we went. It was taxing, but that's what training is supposed to be.

My friends Andy and Sarah Proft in the 2016 Solstice Parade.
Photo: Owen Duncan

I was Ralph's player-coach. In semi-pro baseball, there are player-coaches. They are young enough to play with younger players, but sufficiently older and more experienced to actually be the coaches of the team. When I played baseball, I played with one or two of them. Now I'm a stilting player-coach, because I'm also always in training, to see if I can continue rising up on stilts.

Ralph first got up on my starter stilts, from ages and ages ago. They are heavy, at 8.2 pounds each. I didn't think he'd be able to do it, and I told him so. I said, "It's a real long shot; I don't think it's

Ralph Luikart in the 2016 Solstice Parade. Photo: Owen Duncan

gonna happen, Ralph." That night, I woke up in the middle of the night, and it occurred to me that I didn't want to be discouraging. I decided we could look for some lighter stilts, and the next day I saw, to my amazement, some $300 quality stilts selling for $80 on eBay. I told Ralph I thought we could really make a go of it, and so we embarked.

Ralph performed wonderfully in the parade, as a jolly green giant. He cavorted and skipped around like a man half his age. Every time I looked his way, he had a broad smile. He was obviously in joy, and being carried along by the joy and the support that was coming his way. After our experience together on high, I feel like he's my younger brother, a new member of my stilting family.

When I was a boy growing up, there was a German family of trapeze artists called the Flying Wallendas. When I started stilting I was excited by the notion of the Stilting McGinneses. I hope that I've started a stilting dynasty. Both of my sons, Skye and Zach, are stilters.

Skye and Zach are fine stiltwalkers, and I love to see them on stilts, at ease, in relaxation and joy. As boys, both rose up above the heads of the not-so-tall grown-ups around them, and in no time at all they were cavorting about on stilts taller than mine, calling me "Shorty."

Speaking of "Shorty," when Skye was way too young to rise up on stilts in the Summer Solstice Parade with me, he had the idea of going up the street beside me as the shortest person next to the tallest person, scooting himself along on padded knees! We were all surprised by how far he got. Talk about grit! Since then, whenever he's in the parade, he's over eight feet tall.

Every year, Zach comes up with a great new costume for stilting in the parade. Once he appeared as a lawyer joke: a shark carrying a briefcase and wearing a suit. Another time (my favorite), he dressed as a flamingo, with black legs, a bright pink body, and a neck that went up to a beautifully fashioned papier-mâché head. The head was attached to his shoulders by one of those flexible plastic drainage pipes, and he could move it around on a stick he held in his hands. He strode along, birdlike, dipping the head into the crowd to the delight of children and adults alike.

It has been a blessing to see my grandchildren Helena, 14, and Larkin, 12, rise up and shine on stilts. I imagine their sister Chloe, 4, rising up to join them one day. I hope there will always be at least one of my descendants who loves to rise up on stilts and share joy with the community.

4. AN UPLIFTING LIFE

Stilting need not take place in a celebratory context. Indeed, stilting enhances many other parts of life. As I mentioned earlier, people have been using stilts at work since time immemorial. In fact, the kind of stilts I use are the drywall stilts that people who work on walls and ceilings strap onto their legs, enabling them to work for hours on end without having to constantly climb, descend, and reposition ladders.

Sports are a natural fit for stilting. Of course, since stilts elevate you to great heights, basketball comes to mind. So I've dribbled basketballs on stilts, and I've heard endless jokes about how I must be a basketball player. Stilting could become a part of track and field competitions quite easily. I think a stilts Olympics would be of interest to both athletes and spectators. Stilt racing could involve competing individuals and relay teams over various distances, matching competitors wearing stilts of varying heights. How about the 400 meters, or the mile, or the marathon on stilts? Shot put, discus, javelin... the whole decathlon. Even bicycle races, using a special kind of bicycle, could be done.

There's no reason to perform on the old clunkers I use. Special racing stilts could be designed for the sport, made out of a very lightweight, high-strength material. Perhaps a number of competing designs might be made and sold in sporting goods stores. Kangaroo stilts would be perfectly suited to athletic events, races, basketball, and the like. I once saw a woman racing around on these, running

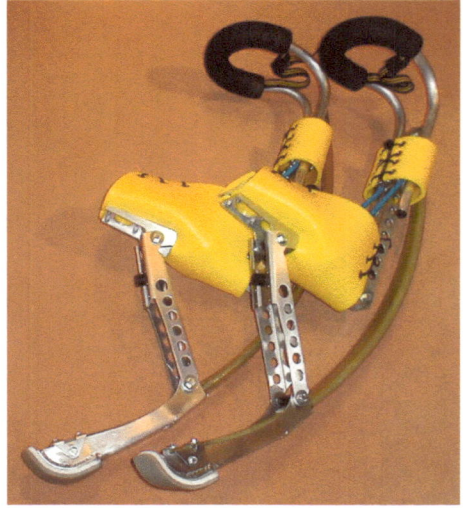

One of many kinds of kangaroo or jumping stilts. Photo: Mmishak

on the grass at the courthouse lawn. It was her first time up on stilts, and off she went, bouncing like a gazelle. "This is a great workout!" she yelled as she raced along.

You couldn't do swimming events or tackling sports, but nearly anything else could be done. Soccer, tennis, badminton... Other possibilities will occur to you. Just imagine yourself on stilts, doing what you love to do. Imagine yourself, too, designing and building the stilts that you'd be on.

A long time ago, I predicted that somebody would roller-skate on stilts, and lo and behold, recently I saw a man roller-skating on stilts online. How beautiful it is, roller-skating on stilts! You can probably Google and find just about anything on stilts. Speaking of just about anything, I was once romantically propositioned while up on my stilts, but the details of that story belong in another kind of book.

More suitable for this book is the story of how I popularized the use of stilts in higher education, at least in the sense that whenever I have risen up on my stilts at the University of California, Santa Barbara, it has generally been a popular and memorable occurrence.

"Let there be light" is the motto of the University of California. By rising up on stilts as a faculty member there, I intend to expand the motto to include joy and fun. As a teacher in higher education, I believe it is my responsibility to do all I can to inspire and foster elevated awareness and understanding, and occasionally rising up on stilts in the classroom is among the ways I have to do that.

Rising up on stilts is a wonderful way to provide highlights and overviews that tend to be remembered and thought about more carefully than if I were to deliver them merely standing in my shoes. I use the stilts in the classroom to draw attention to concepts, ideas, and thoughts, as a means of really attracting the attention of my students not to myself but to the very idea that we don't have to just do things in too serious a manner, we can lighten up and look deeply at the same time. Serious matters should be considered both seriously and with a good dose of levity, especially in the field of environmental studies, because it can be so dispiriting to learn what we're doing to the well-being of the planet.

I also rise up to communicate with administrators, just to lighten things up, to give them something to laugh about as they conduct their serious business. For about 20 years, I kept a tradition at the beginning of every academic year (a tradition I mean to carry on now that I've returned to teaching on campus). Departing my office on stilts, I'd walk across campus to the university's administrative offices at Cheadle Hall. I'd duck into the elevator and go all the way up to the top floor, into the chancellor's office, to greet another higher-up.

There was an outer office with a few desks, and the people at the desks would look up, smile, laugh, and then announce me. I made these traditional visits to Robert Huttenback, Daniel G. Aldrich, Barbara Uehling, and most recently to Henry T. Yang.

Chancellor Yang really got a kick out of it when he came out of his office and saw me standing there. Some of the others whom I visited in that office regarded me with dour expressions or thin smiles, and I got the feeling that they thought it was mighty weird for a member of the faculty to be doing such a thing, bordering on the outrageous. But Henry has a lively sense of humor, and he rose to the occasion to greet me as one higher-up to another, and he, his staff, and I all had a wonderful few minutes going through the many ways to describe what we were doing there together on the very top floor.

I would say things like, "Well, I thought I'd hang out here for a bit, in the upper echelons. So this is higher education at its best! Top floor... with all the higher-ups gathered here." Then I would look around and say, "Well, actually, you're not so high up after all." Then I'd invite them all to consider walking on stilts occasionally on campus. Consider designating an occasion on which everyone—students, staff, faculty, administrators—might be encouraged to rise up on stilts, an occasion to affirm and demonstrate that levity has an important place in higher education.

I have also walked on stilts here and there within the corridors of the Santa Barbara County Courthouse, City Hall, and the County Administration Building, where at one time I had frequently appeared, wearing regular shoes, as a lawyer and advocate. People there didn't expect to witness the sight of an eight-foot-tall man with an amiable smile walking through the solemn corridors of power as if nothing at all were out of the ordinary. Initial shock quickly gave way to smiles, chuckles, and happy repartee.

Once I appeared on my stilts in a coat and tie in the courtroom of my friend Judge Jim Slater. I timed it so that when I walked into the courtroom and stood in the back, he was out of the room on recess. When he entered he saw me, but I think his secretary had tipped him off before, because he said very quickly, "Ladies and gentlemen, before we resume, it should be noted that the tall fellow there in the back is Marc McGinnes, an attorney, if you can believe it. Perhaps, Mr. McGinnes, you can tell us just what you're doing here."

I said, "I've got a case that I'm taking to the highest court in the land! Is this it?"

Jim laughed and said, "No, I think you're in the wrong place. But thank you for your visit."

The room was filled with laughter as I made my exit, wondering how the judge would restore order in his courtroom.

On several occasions, I appeared before the Board of Supervisors on stilts in order to promote the Summer Solstice Celebration. A surprising number of people watch the proceedings of the Board of Supervisors on community television, so I would appear during the week before the event, to remind the board and viewers that it was coming up.

When I first started wearing stilts, I did a lot of walking out and about in the community to practice. I began going inside stores and other places, ducking carefully beneath the doorways and acting upon entering as if nothing were out of the ordinary. I still practice like this as parade season approaches. I just walk along regularly, because I'm not particularly trying to get attention, but it's still fun to watch people's reactions. Some people will look at me and smile and say hello. Children are just magnetized, because it's like I'm a friendly giant. Often, parents will ask their kids, "Would you like to go up and

Up, up she rises. Photo: John Barron

say hi to the giant? Would you like to be up there, to look around up there?" If the child says OK, then the parent will hand the child up to me. I'll reach down, there's a wonderful moment of trust and joy, the actual physical lifting up of this little person, and then we look out together, just looking around at this new world without speaking.

Those are wonderful moments. I have a great picture commemorating such a moment with my son Zach—who's now taller than me—when he was a small child, his mother having handed him up to me. One year in the parade, a man handed up his daughter to me, saying, "You don't remember this, of course, but my mother handed me up to you!" If I had died right then (well, not with the baby in my arms, of course!), that would have been a good time to go. There would have been a big cycle completed right then and there.

While the idea of dying doing what you love is attractive, I wouldn't really want to die in the parade. Imagine the headlines! What a downer. I wouldn't want something like that to happen in front of people, especially children. If I die on stilts, I would prefer that it happen during an enjoyable stroll all alone, along a packed-earth

Uplifting joy. Photo: Pete Evans

pathway through an orchard of blossoming trees, my having become carried away by the beauty all around, tripping, falling, and cracking my head on the ground. Gone, just like that.

Even if I don't wind up dying on stilts, I can see myself being buried in them in an extra-long coffin, laid to rest at full length beneath a headstone befittingly tall. I can also see myself being cremated wearing a pair of my wooden stilts, our ashes mingling, to be sprinkled here and there, from dust and sawdust to dust.

If there really are pearly gates of some kind, I'm certain that you could walk right through them wearing stilts and be welcomed in with a chuckle and a smile. For me, stilting is a way of knowing and expressing the love in my heart, and that opportunity is a blessing for which I am deeply grateful in this lifetime. If there is an afterlife, I'm pretty sure that stilting will be among the blessings in abundance there.

The Stilting McGinneses: Skye, Zach, and Marc (left to right).
Photo: Kathy Snow

Grandson Larkin and friend Niko in 2015 Solstice Parade.
Photo: Kathy Snow

Solstice family zaniness. Photo: Eric Isaacs/EMI Photography

Three generations of stilting McGinneses. Photo: Isaac Hernández Herrero

In joy on high. Photo: Seyburn Zorthian

FROM ANOTHER PERSPECTIVE

When I see Marc on stilts, I see a joyful spirit ushering in celebration, revelry, and community. Since my first experience of Santa Barbara's Summer Solstice Parade in 1991, and for every single one before that, Marc has appeared at the start of the parade on his stilts, dressed in white, with rainbow colored ribbons flowing from the wreath on his head and radiant joy flowing from his face.

His jolly smile is an invitation—never vain, yet full of pride at the glory our community creates for this special day of the year. His sunny Solstice smile is a reminder that we all belong, we all have a part in this jubilant exultation of art, of nature, and of each other. He clearly enjoys the energy, the attention... but his enjoyment is not egotistical—it is generous, abundant. He is an open channel, inviting all to tune in to his festive frequency and jam to the music that comes from deep within us all.

— Queen Justine (aka Justine Sutton), Summer Solstice celebrant

As a stilter in the Summer Solstice, I felt I was really honoring all of the people who came out to show off their costumed bodies, as I could see so much from my vantage point! Well, maybe it was more about my sightseeing... but regardless, it's great to interact with people from the elevated perspective of stilts.

— Skye McGinnes, stiltwalker

Marc has been the opening symbol of the Solstice Parade, the person who was in all the parades, and for me personally, seeing him was the assurance that all was well, and things were going to proceed as they had for the many, many previous years. I also looked forward to seeing him in the park afterward, and he always gave me the biggest hug and congratulations. Thank you, Marc, for being the beacon for Solstice... always standing above the rest.

— Claudia Bratton, artist, Executive Director,
Santa Barbara Summer Solstice Celebration, 1999-2015

My life was completely changed by the Summer Solstice Parade. At the tender age of 22, it prompted a drive in me to pursue my dream of dance and theatre. One of the greatest things about this parade has been its Elevation. Solstice doesn't just go from curb to curb; it goes skyward as well. I know on that magic day in 1980, what struck and excited me was its LOFT. Big balloon arches, banners, larger than life puppets and of course, STILTWALKERS!

I cannot express enough the joy and creative boost I received and continue to receive now. And what a joy to live in a community that values its artists the way Santa Barbara does! We all know and inspire each other here, and it makes our community joyful and colorful. I was born here and for goodness sake, I truly hope I die here. Thank you, Marc, for dancing up in the air and inspiring us all!

— Steven Lovelace, former Artistic Director, Santa Barbara
Summer Solstice Celebration; Director, Santa Barbara Dance Arts

Seeing Marc each Solstice, the tallest person with the grandest smile, always makes my temperature rise, my heart sing, and my soul delight. I have loved him forever, and to watch him, gaily costumed, stunning shining face, and stooping to conquer us all, is one of the best reasons to watch the Summer Solstice Parade. Occasionally he will bend so low as to plant a kiss on my lips.

— Gail Rappaport, Mediator, Mediation Center, Santa Barbara

After admiring Marc for years as he led the Solstice Parade up State Street in Santa Barbara, I finally met him face-to-face. Like a charming leprechaun with a mischievous smile, Marc lit up when he talked about his experience on stilts. After much cajoling and a little bargaining, I convinced him to coach me. As a result of his excellent tutelage and many long hours learning to dance on stilts, I had the pleasure of joining him at the front of the Santa Barbara Solstice Parade in 2016. Marc lit up the street with his contagious grin and I couldn't stop smiling as we danced our way back and forth from side to side and round in circles. It is a day I shall never forget, and I have my good friend Marc to thank for the extraordinary experience.

— Ralph Luikart, stiltwalker

I spent 20 years on the bench, including five frantic years on the Municipal Court, dealing with an enormous number of cases on a daily basis where a sense of the humorous side of both chaos and redundant DUI trials came in handy. Your startling entry into my courtroom in Superior Court stands out as one of the funniest.

I can clearly remember that day. At first, there was some commotion at the doorway to my courtroom, with my bailiff (Jim Brandlin, now a Superior Court judge in Los Angeles County) and another person trying to hold the door open for what appeared at first to be a gigantic person trying to duck down low enough to wedge his way through the opening. I didn't know what to make of the situation. All eyes in the room were watching, transfixed by the scene. Slowly, the figure became upright and, as I remember it, placed a top hat on his head. There you were, making your appearance in the "high court," mounted on stilts covered in extra long pants and (again, as I recall) wearing a frock coat. The room roared with laughter, as I did, too. Great memories!

— Hon. James M. Slater, Judge,
Santa Barbara Superior Court (ret.)

As an undergraduate student in Marc's environmental law classes, it was an incredible inspiration to be his student. He was a spark for my passion for environmental organizing. One of the annual events I coordinated was Isla Vista Earth Day, a day long festival of music, performances, activities, and community in Isla Vista's iconic Anisq'Oyo' Park. Often, several thousand students would attend throughout the day, but it was quite rare to ever see a professor join us. However, Marc was an exception, and year after year he would join us in the park. It was quite a sight to see Marc with us, dancing in the crowd, hanging out with all of us, and then launching up on his stilts and walking around. Flower crown and white clothes flowing, he spread an energy of love and peace. His subjects in class were heavy: pollution, trespass, nuisance, public process, property rights, environmental laws... but his spirit is much lighter, and nothing brings that more into focus than celebrating Earth Days, Summer Solstices and other community events on stilts, with a giant smile lighting up his face.

— Ariana Katovich, former student, consultant

On the longest day of the year for about fifteen years, I grew 20 inches and morphed into various creatures, characters or weird shapes. I was a Stilt Walker in the Santa Barbara Solstice Parade, one of three, with Doug Smith and Evelyn Jacob. It is interesting to consider what brought us the most joy. Was it striding high above the colorful crowds with a stunning view of the Ensembles? Or was it the creation and building of our costumes?

First we were green Praying Mantises, with cleverly jointed limbs (my all time favorite), and then silver aliens with huge bulbous foam heads. It was a miracle we made it up State Street intact, with our heads inside these bobble heads, drastically limiting our vision and balance. "Tallerinas" found us decked out in pastel tutus as we pliéd and swooped, pushing the ballet bar uphill. Do you know that State Street is an uphill walk? Doug was particularly stunning with his hairy chest.

Frankly I've lost count of all the costumes, over all the years we spent on stilts. Stilt walking was a challenge—physical and mental. It became a passion. But most of all it was outrageously exhilarating and FUN.

— Heidi Schulz, stiltwalker

The first time up high was like the first time on an airplane. When you look down you see the world so small... well, maybe not that small, but you get the picture. When you're getting up it feels a little bit hazardous, but once you're used to it you feel like a giant, like you can conquer anything. The first few steps are real eye openers; you see the world as a whole new place. It's like you're learning to walk again.

— Nikolai Proft, age 11, stiltwalker

My first exposure to stilting was through my 10-year-old son. He'd been invited to a park to stilt with a friend and the friend's grandfather, Marc McGinnes. Marc provided the stilts at the park, and my son was able to borrow them afterward. The goal was that if he practiced, he and his friends could stilt in the kids' Earth Day parade. What a lovely invitation for my child, an afternoon in the park with friends trying something new, for free! Invitation accepted.

Marc asked me help supervise, so I joined them. The spacious, grassy, obstacle free park was chosen to cushion any potential falls. Marc kindly set out to give instructions and the boys were excited to get up, not thinking about how it might play out. They each jockeyed for a place on the picnic table where they could strap into the stilts. Marc's grandson was up and moving instantly, having done it many times before. The other two boys were right behind. My son took to it right away, and his gait grew more confident with each step.

No sooner were the kids up on stilts and feeling confident, when Marc enforced the first and most important rule: no locking bodies or making contact with other people while on stilts! It was a swift ruling by the McGinnes patriarch, because the boys started using their balancing staffs like swords. As the boys' confidence grew, the second rule was explained: fall down. Forcing a fall is counter-intuitive when you have the sensation of being a mile high. But once you muster the courage to fall, the fears melt and your higher stance become the new normal.

After the lesson in the park, my son took to practicing the stilts around the house, which eventually led to my husband and I trying it too. This experience has given rise to a new family ritual of stilting in the Summer Solstice Parade.

Each year as we prepare I'm surprised with myself, as I never would have guessed I'd be stilting in a parade. You see, I'm mostly an introvert and I don't like crowds. Yet somehow being on stilts exempts me from this limitation. Being "up" allows me to be a part of the festivities without having to be "in" the crowd. It's like the sea of people on both sides of the street are my bolsters, and the perceived separation creates a cocoon. I'm effortlessly able to stride among a mass of strangers—an introvert at heart with a temporary, extrovert's exemption. At the end of the the parade it's so disappointingly normal to be "down."— Sarah Proft, stiltwalker

I t has been my pleasure to assist Marc with costuming for the Summer Solstice Celebration for the past several years. It has pushed my talents to new heights! He is a master at sharing his joy and generosity.

— Traci Jackson, Costume Designer,
Santa Barbara Summer Solstice Celebration

O ne of the inspirational moments of my professional career was to witness the great legal, ethical mind of Marc, towering on his stilts over the County Board of Supervisors during their political deliberation years back. Imagine the divine effect of Counselor McGinnes, waving hands and gesticulating, as to how that powerful body simply could not but consider the sanity offered from his ethereal perch! Of course they were taken aback, and perhaps defensive, as well. After all, Marc was a Planning Commissioner himself, and familiar with the vagaries and drama of the protesting public. So how could he presume to "get on his high horse" (in this case, a two-legged Trojan Horse) to emphatically remind the public representatives of their necessary mindfulness? But of course, that was exactly Marc's strategy! And a memorable, effective one at that!

— David Stone, environmental planning consultant

For many years I had the pleasure of facilitating a circus camp for 8–13 year-olds in Santa Barbara. We focused on the old European and multicultural shamanic clowning traditions, mostly to help students develop their voices, bodies, imaginations and performance skills, which help them to grow both as artists and as citizens. One of the most simple, yet rewarding skills we offered was stiltwalking.

For small people to get their head above those around them (especially the adults), it was always a thrill to watch. Immediate confidence was built by facing their fear and mastering the skill, and then, when they looked out from that new place, the world presented itself anew... perspective reached!

Since then, I've used stilts large and small to build characters in the theatre. We now have a Cyclops in our production of Homer's *Odyssey*, who stalks the stage on jumping stilts, giving him a real sense of animality and offering him an impressive three-foot rise.

Stilts are also, as exampled by Mr. McGinnes, a fabulous way to parade. He has been inspiring us for years with his powerful spirit in the Santa Barbara Solstice Celebration, always colorful, always beaming with joy! Thanks for your inspiration, my kindred, high heeled brother!

— Michael Andrews, Executive Artistic Director,
Boxtales Theatre Company

Marc opens up and blossoms when he's on stilts. He takes great pleasure in the enjoyment he gives to others, especially the children, who always love the attention of such a tall magical man. He lets the music dance him up the parade route, being as much fulfilled in the process as the people watching.

— Seyburn Zorthian, artist

There's nothing like towering high above everyone else, doing a precarious feat that 99.9% of people would never dream of doing. It's a wonderful feeling, and since most of the people viewing me in the Santa Barbara Summer Solstice Parade are looking up from the perspective of their seats along the curb, I appeared even taller.

In my first parade on stilts I was joined by my friends Heidi and Doug, also on stilts, as a Praying Mantis ensemble. We had long green tails which moved as we walked and many arms and legs. I still run into people who tell me that it was their favorite costume ensemble ever.

For the next five years, I designed a costume and ensemble that would always include me on stilts. Heidi, Doug and I had an outer space ensemble with capes that lit up with blinking lights. One year the theme of the parade was "Hot," so I made a costume of flames with hot red and orange colors.

The next year we did the Tallerinas ensemble. We went as oversize ballerinas with our stilts covered with thick padding that made our legs look grotesquely huge. We did our ballerina exercises, holding onto a long, elevated ballet bar, while slowly walking up State St. at the same time. Our friend Doug was the funniest ballerina, and I almost fell from laughing when I saw him in his blue tutu with his hairy arms.

My last year on stilts I went as a fortune teller. Mindy and I constructed a high table with a magic ball on it, and there were fake arms coming from my shoulders that held the ball. That way, I could hold onto the inner railings of the table and push my way up the street.

I always enjoyed making it look like there was a reason that I was on stilts. I liked to incorporate them into the ensemble so they became a part of the story.

— Evelyn Jacob, stiltwalker

My creative interests brought me into costuming. I was exploring new shapes, and I had the idea of creating tall, elongated characters. A fellow artist had a pair of drywall stilts and suggested I try them out to achieve the effect I was looking for. I never had attempted to stiltwalk prior to that time, so drywall stilts were the perfect solution, providing me with stability and up to 38 inches of additional height.

First came The Wizard, a character I created for a Winter Solstice event. He was eight feet plus tall, with long hair from a bald-pated cap and long mustache. The Wizard got around, I had a lot of fun parading for several years with him.

I'm not sure which character came next, but I think it was the Pierrot clown costume my Solstice Godmother made me. I had been the workshop director for Summer Solstice Celebration that year. I helped everyone else complete their costumes and ensembles, and that left me with little time to think about my own costume. Nan Parsons was running the costume shop, and surprised me with a beautiful Pierrot clown costume for me to wear up the parade route. She even made the costume a pair of "short pants" to wear with the costume when not on stilts.

That was also the year I fell on the parade route. I pushed my luck trying to do a "shuffle-ball-chain" tap step. After I fell, I was surrounded by people checking on my welfare. I felt okay. So, I rolled over to my back and a crowd of people lifted me back up, and off I went to complete the parade. I had a fractured wrist and I never wanted to fall again.

I had known Evelyn and Heidi through the Solstice workshop for a few years. They were great participants in the workshop, always coming up with creative ensembles with great artistic expression. We collaborated well. I think during the first brainstorming session we came up with the Praying Mantis. The concept unfolded beautifully, and what a crowd pleaser it turned out to be! The sight of the three of us giant green mantises moving up the street was unforgettable.

I think it was the following year that Rich McLaughlin got in on the act, and produced another stilt ensemble called the Alien Eyeballs, with giant single eyeballs on slinky, columnar bodies (we looked a lot like giant walking penises). I do believe we had at least seven or eight people on stilts that year.

There was a revamp of Evelyn and Heidi's costumes where they became space aliens, and I followed behind as their pet mantis. We used those costumes in both West Hollywood and San Luis Obispo Mardi Gras. Rich was playing with el-wire that year, and produced a giant robot backpack puppet that he wore in addition to his stilts to add bulk to his huge height.

In my opinion, the best of our stilt costumes came last, and I had very little to do with them. It was Solstice time again, and I was engrossed in my family. A week before the parade, I held my grandmother as she passed from this life. My father was actively dying and I would hold my father a month later as he passed. Needless to say, emotionally speaking, I had a full plate.

I had no time for the workshop, but I agreed to be in the parade if a costume was provided. Evelyn, Heidi and Mindy made the "Tallerinas." They concealed our stilts within the very thick legs of the ballerina costumes. It was a brilliant concept.

I remember showing up to the parade route and they had a lot of options for my costume; not having had the chance for a proper fitting prior to parade day.

Our costumes usually incorporated some sort of pole or support device. None of us were interested in falling and hurting ourselves. This year Evelyn, Heidi, and Mindy ingeniously used a ballet bar for the Tallerinas to support ourselves as we moved up the street.

We were a big hit, and I remember very little of it. I lost myself in this giant oversized big girl and let loose on my grief, while grunting, doing squats and perfecting my dance on the way up the parade route. Ironically, it was several years before I even saw pictures of the full ensemble with the three of us in the air and Mindy on the ground, acting as Ballet Teacher trying to manage these three very unlikely cumbersome Tallerinas.

— Douglas Smith, stiltwalker

My grandfather Papou [Marc] taught me how to walk on stilts when I was seven or eight years old. I was a bit nervous at first, but after taking a few steps while holding his hand, I felt comfortable enough to let go. It was in the park downtown, and walking on the grass was a good way to begin. Later on, I walked with Papou in the Summer Solstice Parade, and that was scarier because of all the people and the hard surface of the street. My dad was my spotter, and I am glad he was there. Papou got tripped up and fell, and that kinda freaked me out. Papou was okay, and he hardly missed a beat, and we continued on together for a couple of blocks until I asked my dad to help me get down so I could watch the rest of the parade with him.

— Helena McGinnes, age 14, stiltwalker

'm glad to be part of a family of stiltwalkers. When Papou [Marc] asked me if I wanted to try, I asked him if I could invite some friends to try, too. Papou has lots of stilts, so three of us got together at the park on the grass, and he showed all of us what to do. He asked who wanted to go first, and I volunteered. It was easy, like he said it would be. Pretty soon, the three of us were running around and chasing each other. I've had fun being in the Solstice Parade and the Earth Day parade.

— Larkin McGinnes, age 12, stiltwalker

tiltwalking is an activity that I recommend to anyone who is physically able to walk (raised wheelchairs hopefully coming soon!). I had the benefit of learning young, but it's anyone's game. Moving around up there is just such a rewarding experience, and so easy to learn. Go find a pair and see for yourself!

— Zach McGinnes, occasional giant

Photo: Isaac Hernández Herrero

ACKNOWLEDGMENTS

It took a team to put this book together: Ilene Segalove, who refused to let me give up. Nancy Black and Isaac Hernández Herrero at Mercury Press International, who enabled me to keep on and made it real. And Owen Duncan, who showed me my voice. My gratitude to them is boundless.

I am also grateful beyond measure for the love and support I receive from my immediate and extended families, especially for those who rise up with me as the Stilting McGinneses. Sharing these times has been among my greatest joys.

And I must not forget my friends, colleagues and fellow citizens, particularly those with whom I work and play in the Summer Solstice, Community Environmental Council, Environmental Defense Center, UCSB, Gaviota Coast Conservancy and other communities.

I am uplifted by so many beautiful souls who nourish and sustain my spirit whether I wear my stilts, my shoes, no shoes, or nothing at all. Thank you to all those who have stood for me and with me, and provided guidance, love and support. Please take this moment to see me seeing you. I offer you my deepest thanks and blessings.

www.ingramcontent.com/pod-product-compliance
Lightning Source LLC
LaVergne TN
LVHW010016070426
835511LV00001B/8